The Jessie and John Danz Lectures

THE JESSIE AND JOHN DANZ LECTURES

The Human Crisis, by Julian Huxley
Of Men and Galaxies, by Fred Hoyle
The Challenge of Science, by George Boas
Of Molecules and Men, by Francis Crick
Nothing But or Something More, by Jacquetta Hawkes
How Musical Is Man?, by John Blacking
Abortion in a Crowded World: The Problem of Abortion with Special Reference to India, by S. Chandrasekhar
World Culture and the Black Experience, by Ali A. Mazrui
Energy for Tomorrow, by Philip H. Abelson
Plato's Universe, by Gregory Vlastos
The Nature of Biography, by Robert Gittings

THE
NATURE
OF
BIOGRAPHY

by
ROBERT
GITTINGS

UNIVERSITY OF
WASHINGTON PRESS
SEATTLE

Library of Congress Cataloging in Publication Data
Gittings, Robert.
The nature of biography.

(The Jessie and John Danz lectures)
1.   Biography (as a literary form) 2.   England –
Biography. 1. Title.
CT21.G5   808'.066'92   78–3136
ISBN 0–295–95604–6

Contents

To Bill and Judy Matchett
my hosts in Seattle

Acknowledgements

The author and publishers wish to thank the following for permission to reproduce copyright material:

Chatto & Windus Ltd and Harcourt Brace Jovanovich, Inc. for the extract from *Eminent Victorians* by Lytton Strachey; Faber & Faber Ltd and Random House, Inc. for the extracts from *Collected Poems* by W. H. Auden: John A. Garraty and Random House, Inc. for the extracts from *The Nature of Biography* by John A. Garraty; Constable Publishers for the extracts from *The Reason Why* by Cecil Woodham-Smith; A. D. Peters & Co. Ltd for the extract from *A Hidden Life* by Hugh Trevor-Roper.

The Jessie and John Danz Lectures

In October, 1961, Mr John Danz, a Seattle pioneer, and his wife, Jessie Danz, made a substantial gift to the University of Washington to establish a perpetual fund to provide income to be used to bring to the University of Washington each year '. . . distinguished scholars of national and international reputation who have concerned themselves with the impact of science and philosophy on man's perception of a rational universe'. The fund established by Mr and Mrs Danz is now known as the Jessie and John Danz Fund, and the scholars brought to the University under its provisions are known as Jessie and John Danz Lecturers or Professors.

Mr Danz wisely left to the Board of Regents of the University of Washington the identification of the special fields in science, philosophy, and other disciplines in which lectureships may be established. His major concern and interest were that the fund would enable the University of Washington to bring to the campus some of the truly great scholars and thinkers of the world.

Mr Danz authorized the Regents to expend a portion of the income from the fund to purchase special collections of books, documents, and other scholarly materials needed to reinforce the effectiveness of the extraordinary lectureships and professorships. The terms of the gift also provided for the publication and dissemination, when this seems appropriate, of the lectures given by the Jessie and John Danz Lecturers.

Through this book, therefore, another Jessie and John Danz Lecturer speaks to the people and scholars of the world, as he has spoken to his audiences at the University of Washington and in the Pacific Northwest community.

Introduction

This book is based, with very little alteration, on the Jessie and John Danz Lectures, delivered in the University of Washington, Seattle, in June 1977, under the title of 'The Art and Science of Biography'. The founder of these lectures, Mr Danz, had wished them to be connected with his own 'special and deep interest . . . in man's perception of a rational universe'. The nature of biography seemed, both to myself and to those who so generously appointed me to this lectureship, at least to partake of this perception, even though it might often be expressed in the study of frequently irrational human behaviour. As well as this more philosophic background, the lectures provided me with a chance to express the beliefs of a working biographer, based on a quarter of a century of such work, and for that alone I owe a lasting debt to the committee of the Graduate Faculty which nominated me, and the Board of Regents which appointed me.

For the book, and the lectures on which it is based,

must often carry with them a personal view, which has something to do with the origins of myself as a biographer. Biography, with me, arose out of my attempts at poetry, and, indeed, as this book suggests, I still see a relationship between the two arts. To add to the many phrases which try to define the nature of biography, it is for me poetry with a conscience. In 1950, at which date I had not the least intention ever to write biography, I produced a book of verse, whose title-poem, *Wentworth Place*, was a series of impressions in verse of the two years spent by the poet Keats in the Hampstead house of that name. This sequence, each part headed by an extract from Keats's letters, and often using adapted phrases from the same source, tried to reconstruct imaginatively his life during this period, when all his greatest poems were written. Like all poetry, it did not pretend to be a literal interpretation but rather a symbolic one; yet the symbols I used were the facts of his life. When this was printed, some stirring of artistic conscience, or perhaps my previous training as an historian, made me question my own right to present Keats's life in this way, without having ascertained the truth on which my poetic assumptions were based. Did the Keats I had conceived ever exist? Out of that question arose my subsequent involvement in the writing of biography, and the attempt to find convincing outward warrant for the inner events of life, particularly the life of a creative artist such as Keats and, later, Hardy.

This idiosyncratic start to my career as a biographer may help to explain one or two features in this book. Though planned as a comprehensive view of biographical writing by English writers on English subjects, it has some features individual to my own work, which perhaps need mentioning. Its three parts are entitled, as were the original lectures, 'Past History', 'Present Practice', and 'Paths of Progress' respectively. Although I have tried to make my treatment of these sub-titles as comprehensive as possible, it is obvious that a great deal of selection has had to take place. Where examples and quotations had to be given to illustrate some point in the history of biography, or the practice of some particular form of biography, I have tried to choose what seemed to me the best possible instance. A much larger book would be needed to do justice to the whole sweep of biographical writing, and I can only hope that what I have omitted will not seem to be doing injustice to the many fine biographers I have had to treat in this way. Nor is my treatment and interpretation of their work, I am conscious, always that of the writers themselves. Where this has occurred, I can only say that my quotation from, and appreciation of the biographies cited in this book, is everywhere informed by my admiration for the authors' skill and penetration in that most difficult of all tasks, the true presentation of their fellow human beings. Finally, though I have tried to spread the net wide, I am conscious that I have often dredged up from my own experience as a biographer what seemed convincing examples of biographical practice, if I could not find better ones in the works of others. Hence the reader will undoubtedly find instances of the biographer's problems and methods drawn from my own processes in writing the lives of Keats and of Hardy. In fact, the book proper actually begins with a quotation from those letters of Keats which were my starting-point as a practising biographer.

I
Past History

---

*Above all, they are very shallow people who take
everything literal. A Man's life of any worth is
a continual allegory – and very few eyes can see the
Mystery of his life . . . a life like the scriptures,
figurative.*

These words, by the poet John Keats, should stand
at the head of every attempt to define the art and
science of biography: at the head, even more, of every
attempt to write a biography of anybody. They form
both a warning and a challenge, and have, in Keats's
own phrase, their own portion of mystery. Strictly
interpreted, they could condemn very many biographers as 'very shallow people'. For the effort to
'take everything literal', in one sense, that is, to rely
and to proceed only on established fact, proven historically or scientifically, is surely one of the corner-
stones of biography, as we have arrived at it today.
It is a large step to demand every biographer to take,

from the literal, factual truth of events in the life of his subject, to this further process in 'a Man's life of any worth', that is, to interpret the facts in the form of what Keats calls 'a continual allegory', which 'very few eyes can see': in other words, the process of what we may call Art.

Yet that is the point to which, I believe, modern biography has come: that like so many of the casual sparks that Keats struck off – 'particles of light in a great darkness', he himself called them – this definition is a prophetic one, over 150 years ahead of its time. If this is so, it incidentally poses one of the chief paradoxes of life-writing or biography. This is the fact that, while a minute observation and study of the time of the subject's life is essential, the biographer must reckon that many people have not essentially lived in the historic time which their lives span. They are often historically behind it or, like Keats in this instance, ahead of it. Though an examination of contemporary ideas, history, and science must be made, and often reveals much, it is a fallible guide, for this reason: that men and women may only partly and perhaps inessentially live in the time and place they appear physically to inhabit. Every biography, even the most material in its methods, is in fact a comment on the human spirit itself.

This, however, is to arrive too early at the actual practice and scope of biography as it has become at the present day. This first section is mainly concerned with the past, and with the stages in the progress of bio-graphy to the position it now appears to hold. This history of biography is potentially a vast subject, on which I must impose some necessary limitations. I shall be dealing mainly with biography written in, or trans-lated accessibly into, English, and in most instances originating in England. I do not think there are so many differences in life-writing in the English-speaking world that one cannot deduce useful patterns in spite of this limitation. In fact, it may helpfully emphasize, in' many ways, continuity and progress, in spite of some local accidents of history, to a point where, I believe, biography has become one of the most satisfying and established achievements of our present age.

First, then, a few general principles. The quotation from Keats's letter lays stress not only on the symbolic mystery, but on the measurable worth of a person's life – 'a Man's life of any worth'. To make a study of such a life, still more to interest others in the results of such study, one must believe that the life of an indivi-dual can, in fact, have any such worth. 'Man's sociality of Nature,' wrote Carlyle, 'evinces itself in the unspeak-able delight he takes in Biography.' The somewhat curious phrase 'unspeakable delight' certainly describes Carlyle's own feeling, and certainly his own method of writing biography. In fact, Carlyle is so excited – there is no other word for it – by his chosen subject, whether it be a Frederick the Great or a Cromwell, that he cannot keep himself out of the historical background he designs for his hero. He is there all the time, in the crowd of spectators, and not only in the crowd, but leading it, its cheerleader, its spokesman: pointing, plucking us by the elbow, nudging us, in case we should carelessly have missed anything. In modern parallel, he is your neighbour, with whom you are watching a re-run of the television show which he has seen but which you haven't, whose enthusiasm is so great that he keeps telling you what to look for, and that the little fellow who seems to be trailing last on the track in the Olympic event is, in fact, just the man who is going to come through with a burst in the last lap and win the 10,000 metres.

This is not, however, to satirize Carlyle, which is easy enough, as Anthony Trollope first showed in a digressive chapter in *The Warden*, but to dwell for a moment on him as an example of what is perhaps the highest necessity in a biographer. That is, enthusiasm: not necessarily enthusiasm blindly following the person written about, but enthusiasm for the whole daunting pursuit of trying to revive his or her life. It is a task that only the most extreme or even foolhardy enthusiasm can hope to accomplish, in the face of the dead blank of what we do not know and, worse, will never know. One need only think how little we really know of our own close contemporaries and intimates, the essence of their lives: then this, multiplied by the dead distance of past years, by the inevitable loss of the major part of evidence and material, must make us pause doubtfully before we dare to undertake biography. No biographer can ever begin without these doubts. The simple matter of how people talked, to hear their voices, to understand the familiar slang or private family terms, the humour they used, is alarming enough, for a start. Only an initial enthusiasm to believe that the pursuit of life is worthwhile, that life itself in a human being is a desirable subject, can possibly help one to break through the barrier of one's own inevitable inadequacy. That courageous enthusiasm is Carlyle's virtue, and the biographer's inspiration and justification.

So, though Carlyle may be an enthusiastic if vague guide to the original nature of biography, there is no doubt that whatever he means by 'sociality of nature' has something to do with the impulse to write in this form. We may not, like him, interrupt a speech by Cromwell by interjecting 'O brave Oliver' nor, like him again, personally take part in Kaiser Friedrich Wilhelm's Tobacco Parliament, and comment on the jug at the King's elbow with the words 'which I find to consist of excellent thin bitter beer', but his enthusiasm is part of the real stuff of biography. To amend him, one might say that people generally write biography when they are satisfied with the value of life. The poet Arthur Hugh Clough, in his helpful introduction to the so-called Dryden version of Plutarch's Lives, which he himself revised (one of those accessible translations I mentioned), points out that when Plutarch wrote these biographies, in the first century of the Christian era, it was, as Clough says, 'the commencement of the best and happiest age of the great Roman Imperial period'. Clough even sees this reflected in Plutarch's style: 'his language is that of a man happy in himself and in what is around him.' There was, however precariously, a settled Mediterranean world order. The Pax Romana prevailed generally, whatever the domestic evils of imperial government. Men could, however limited the sphere now seems to us, congratulate and celebrate man on existence, a good seed-time for biography.

This is not, of course, to say that biography is nurtured in complacency. It is simply that a generally accepted importance of what people are doing, and can do, in their limited life-span is a favourable condition, a starting-point. One may, like Tolstoi in his *A Confession*, still more in his masterly division of himself into the two autobiographical characters, Prince Andrew and Pierre, in *War and Peace*, come to believe at times that all the actions of a life are useless and unimportant, ending as they must in death. Yet the whole study of a man's attitude to an existence limited by death is itself a major end of biography. If confidence is not quite enough, being vulnerable in this way, curiosity must surely make up another measure of human biography. Keats again, writing to his brother in America a description of his own attitude sitting by the fire in England, added, 'could I see the same thing done of any great Man long since dead it would be a great delight: as to know in what position Shakespeare sat when he began "To be or not to be".' Here again, though curiosity, like complacency, may almost topple over into absurdity, the principle is the same. Stern Shakespeare scholars may say *Hamlet* would be the same whether Shakespeare were sitting or standing; but an intense interest in, and a conviction of the worth of, individual life, can justify and produce the conditions for biography.

Biography begins, then, in one sense or another, in praise. It is also, whether openly or not, didactic praise. Early biographies teach, by example, whatever aspects of the good life its subjects are taken to illustrate. In medieval European times, the Latin Chronicle is almost exclusively the reward of successful secular rulers or of saints. Such chronicles were those refuted some centuries later by Bacon, who reminded us that 'the divine artificer hangs the greatest weight upon the smallest strings'. The chronicles, for all their sudden and sometimes incongruous human touches about the great, were not strictly biography but hagiography. They were written solely to glorify, commemorate, or sometimes to justify the subject of the great man they celebrated, and they were always written about socially or religiously important public figures. They were limited, too, by the usual personality of the biographer. They were almost always written or compiled by some subordinate or official, connected by employment or community with the subject of the work. What they recorded was a mixture of personal knowledge, though often at a very different personal level from their subject, and a kind of guesswork or hearsay to fill in the chronological gaps. Where the author was working within this sphere of personal knowledge, they could often be well-founded and fairly accurate in general terms; where he ventured outside, into other aspects of the subject's life, they could be nonsensical. Asser, bishop of Sherborne, wrote a life of King Alfred, in whose household he had been in the ninth century. A scholar's life of a royal scholar and translator, it is naturally admirable on the king's love of learning and his importance as a pioneer of education. Written by a lover of learning, a monk, it is, as far as we know, accurate on this side of the king. Personal anecdotes of the king as translator have the ring of truth, and can be confirmed. Yet the account of the king as general, and as the commander of campaigns against the invading Danes, though lengthy and circumstantial, are far less satisfactory, and can equally be proved wrong. These were outside the clerical writer's knowledge or experience, gathered haphazard by hearsay and without professional understanding. It is therefore only a true biography of one side of Alfred's life. Above all, like all these early works of life-writing, it is official history, and gives little idea of character. The sole personal touch is when Asser suggests that

Alfred suffered from piles, occupational hazard of scholars.

In the twelfth century, Eadmer, another monk, wrote a life of Anselm which displays a similar set of virtues and weaknesses. He stresses Anselm's holy life, piety, fasts, vigils, miracles, the running of a monastery, all matters about which Eadmer himself knew. He even has several personal anecdotes, some charming, some unconsciously strange. Anselm, according to this biographer, had the power to see through the walls of the monastery, so as to observe what his other monks were doing in their cells, surely a most uncomfortable gift in a Father Superior. This is very well; but of Anselm the statesman, the companion of kings, he says virtually nothing, because he knows so little. There is a certain amount of dubious history, but far more of relics and wonders associated with Anselm after his death than his effect on the Crown and State when he was alive. This weakness in early medieval biography, the fact that the monkish chroniclers only wrote well of matters within their own knowledge, and were ignorant of worldly and public matters outside the cloister walls, is highlighted by that amazing tour-de-force parody of such biography, *Hubert's Arthur* by Rolfe, the so-called Baron Corvo.

The biography of praise, the laudatory chronicle, was a pre-Renaissance idealization of man under God's rule. The Renaissance, with its emphasis on man as individual, ushered in its opposite. Part of this was the biography of denigration, used, after some successful political coup, to demonstrate not the virtues but the vices of the previous régime and its prime leaders. The example most often cited is Sir Thomas More's Tudor biography of the Yorkist Richard III, written about 1513. This, the first biography in English, is perhaps now too often treated as a type of propaganda, the blackening of a past régime so as to gratify the present order. More, as we all know, was an honest, incorruptible man, who hated tyranny of all sorts. His Richard III was equally a warning to his own master, Henry VIII, not to let his own reign get out of hand: a prophetic warning it proved, since More himself, some twenty years later, was to suffer death through his own master's tyranny. Whether propaganda or true biography, however, More's *Richard* brings a new breath into the biographer's art. For one thing, it uses a great deal more first-hand information than had usually been favoured. Its main sources were oral information about Richard's reign from the generation of that time, especially from John Morton, in whose household More had been brought up. The unfinished biography actually ends on what sounds like a realistic firsthand conversation between Morton and the Duke of Buckingham, who is warned that Richard will turn against him eventually, again a prophetic note anticipating More's own fate. It uses facts and anecdotes vouched for by More's own father and father-in-law, and by various personalities of that generation such as Lovell and Urswick. It is a real attempt to recreate a fairly recent time through living, contemporary witness, before memory has faded or become confused. It is, one suspects, often over-simplified and the main characters certainly over-dramatized. Passages read like scenes from a play, as Shakespeare conveniently found when he used it as a source some eighty years later. On the other hand, there is welcome novelty in the treatment of minor characters hitherto neglected in biography of major figures. More portrays Edward IV's generous mistress, Jane Shore, to whom even Shakespeare was unable to allot a speech, quite lengthily.

By the first half of the sixteenth century, at any rate, the tone of voice of the biographer had begun to change. Even when biography in English followed the old laudatory tone of the Latin chronicles, human detail and character kept breaking through. The classic mid-Tudor biographies are those of More himself, by his son-in-law William Roper, and the biography of Wolsey by his gentleman-usher George Cavendish. These works have much in common. Both are by men from the same part of England, noted for its clear-headed, somewhat obstinate honesty, the Suffolk of the later John Constable and other East Anglian painters, who portrayed what they literally saw, but with the individuality of art. It could be said that the welding of scientific observation with imaginative art, which is biography, showed its first sign here,

400 years ago. Both Roper and Cavendish stressed personal knowledge, and where they did not have it, honestly confessed that lack. Cavendish's simple statement of method, 'some part shall be of mine own knowledge, and some of other person's information' may stand as the first straightforward confession made by a biographer to his reading public. Both, of course, were alike in writing within the conventions of their own time. The medieval justification of God's purpose in all things had already given way to the Renaissance wheel-of-fortune image, the rise and fall of a great figure through fate. More's own *Richard III* might well have followed this pattern, if it had been finished. Roper's *More* and Cavendish's *Wolsey* certainly do. Both the success and the fall from it are emphasized, to give dramatic colour. Roper's *More* is a heroic study of a good man beset by material pressures and forces of evil. Cavendish's *Wolsey* is a study of a successful man, whose very success aroused fatal enmity. In both, as so often a generation later with Shakespeare, the fickle multitude, the English people who cheer one day and hiss the next, is denounced. 'O wavering and newfangled multitude,' moralizes Cavendish, though he brings in Anne Boleyn as the arch-traitress, just as Roper brings in Lord Rich, who bore false witness against More at his trial.

There are notable and obvious gaps in both biographies, which a modern writer would never allow. More's *Utopia*, the first thing a present-day reader would wish to hear about, is totally omitted in Roper's account, while Cavendish outdoes this omission by finding no place for Wolsey's contemporary, More himself. Yet it is in convincing, meticulous background detail that both lives point to the future scholarship of biography. The purple passages of Cavendish's account of Wolsey in his grandeur are, admittedly, out of proportion to the work as a whole; but no one would wish to lose this picture of Wolsey, in Cavendish's words,

> *apparelled all in red in the habit of a Cardinal: which*
> *was either of fine scarlet or else of crimson satin, taffeta,*
> *damask or caffa, the best that he could get for money,*
> *and upon his head a round pillion with a neck of black*
> *velvet, set to the same on the inner side. He had also a*
> *tippet of fine sables about his neck, holding in his hand*
> *a very fair orange whereof the meat or substance within*
> *was taken out and filled up again with the part of a*
> *sponge wherein was vinegar and other confections against*
> *the pestilent airs; to the which he most commonly smelt*
> *unto, passing among the press or else when he was*
> *pestered with many suitors.*

This is character, the proud Cardinal's disdain caught in a prose picture. Roper is equally successful with the simple dignity of More, leaving his house and family in Chelsea for the last time on the river Thames.

*And whereas he ever used before, at his departure from
his wife and children, whom he tenderly loved, to have
them bring him to his boat, and there to kiss them all,
and bid them farewell, then would he suffer none of
them forth of the gate to follow him, but pulled the wicket
after him, and shut them all from him : and with an heavy
heart, as by his countenance it appeared, with me and
our four servants there took he his boat towards Lambeth.*

There are many such moments of unconscious
artistry in Tudor biography, emphasizing character
by touches of description, Wolsey proudly smelling
his pomander, More shutting the wicket-gate in lonely
farewell. It is with the seventeenth-century *Lives* by
Isaac Walton – those of Hooker, Herbert, Wotton,
Sanderson, and, in particular, of John Donne – that
the biographer is at work for the first time as a conscious artist. In some ways and attitudes, they are a
regression to the earlier laudatory lives, and the qualifications for praise are even more narrow. They are
lives of High Anglicans in religion, elaborations on the
theme of faith. The literary work of Donne and
Herbert, for example, is hardly mentioned. Yet there
is a conscious attempt to give, from all sources, all the
events of their lives, and to make them a rounded
whole. Walton constructs them far more artfully than
previous life-writers, with a constant eye on the
reader. One literary device is his carefully managed
art of digression, in which he appears to take the

reader into his confidence. The most famous instance is at the point of Donne's last illness: Walton wishes to recapitulate the main features of Donne's life, and yet not spoil the dramatic effect of Donne, for example, virtually preaching his own death-sermon. Walton therefore takes the reader, as it were, personally to Donne's sick-bed, and remarks, with whimsical assurance:

> *My desire is that he may now take some rest and that*
> *before I speak of his death thou [that is, the reader]*
> *wilt not think it an impertinent digression to look back*
> *with me upon some observations of his life, which,*
> *whilst a gentle slumber gives rest to his spirits, may, I*
> *hope, not unfitly exercise thy consideration.*

By making what he afterwards admits is 'my long digression', Walton builds up in the reader a suspense that intensifies the stark nature of Donne's death.

If Walton's digressions are perhaps over-skilfully and self-consciously managed, as foils to set off the main theme, it is possible, as many critics do, to regard the *Brief Lives* of John Aubrey as all digression and no life, or, at the best, a farrago of quaintly expressed but unreliable anecdotes. To do so is to underestimate Aubrey's serious quality. His own life may have been a digression on a theme he never found, but his services to biography were considerable. His passion for first-hand information was real and thorough. He interviewed the widow, brother, and nephew of John

Milton. He obtained evidence about the poetess Katharine Philips, as he says, 'from her cosen Blackett'. He quotes in full a biographical letter from the poet Vaughan's brother. The perennial difficulties of research may lead him to despair – 'what shall one believe!' he cries, on being given two contradictory estimates of Chief Justice Coke's wealth: yet he believes in genuine research, and always confesses and regrets when he is writing with insufficient or lost evidence – ''Tis pity such minutes had not been taken 100 years since,' he exclaims at one point.

The four hundred or so *Lives* are indeed brief. The life of Abraham Wheelock consists of two words only, 'Simple man'; others are, like so much that this amiable procrastinator wrote, mere notes of lives. The longest is under 25,000 words, which we should now consider less than a quarter of an adequate life-study, and many have deliberate gaps, where a fact, a name or date eluded him and was never filled in. Yet Aubrey had many virtues denied to more extensive biographers. He had a sharp eye, a sharper ear for dialogue, and though garrulous himself could get other people to talk naturally. However imperfect, his life-studies are alive. Following Bacon's advice to biographers, he was not afraid to delineate minor or obscure characters. A comparatively unimportant ancestor of my own appears as subject of one of the briefer lives, only of interest to me because he too was a biographer, Henry Isaacson. Aubrey records little more than that this man was snubbed by Charles the First for inaccuracy; but he does it, even with this quite uninfluential person, in a way that reveals the character of this poor man who, Aubrey says, 'was so ashamed at this unlucky rencounter, that he immediately sneak't away and stayd not for praise or reward, both which perhaps he might have had, for his Majestie was well pleased'. Aubrey is the first biographer of the under-privileged, the first biographer of women, who are presented for the first time in his pages not just as the wives, daughters, or mistresses of the heroes of biography, but as themselves, with enough individuality for separate treatment: as in his own words about the Countess of Warwick, 'She needed neither borrowed shades nor reflexive lights to set her off.' In that connection, it is worth noting that Aubrey was an exact contemporary of the two first women biographers, Lucy Hutchinson and Margaret Cavendish, Duchess of Newcastle. Both wrote lives of their husbands, showing qualities which outweigh their partiality, and passages of that minute, human observation which is perhaps the hallmark of the many fine biographies by women writers of our own time.

This care for the little-known or potentially under-rated is shown by the work, itself not well enough known, of Roger North. North wrote biographies of his own three brothers, some time in the second and third decade of the eighteenth century. The best of these is not about the two who distinguished themselves in the world's eye, Dudley and Francis, but about the retiring and short-lived Cambridge scholar, John North. Aubrey had shown what a rich vein of character and eccentricity could be worked from the lives of senior members of the Universities of Oxford and Cambridge, Isaac Barrow, 'pale as the candle he studied by', who preached a sermon of three and a half hours, and then complained that *he* felt tired; or William Harvey, discoverer of the circulation of the blood, who, as Aubrey commented, 'kept a pretty young wench to wayte on him, which I guess he made use of for warmth-sake as King David did'. North's brother John was the archetypal absent-minded professor in real life, who 'in a moonlight night saw someone standing in a white sheet' at the foot of his bed, and after surveying it with nervous alarm, found it was his own towel. He was at my own college, Jesus, where, regrettably, according to his brother, he had 'no relish for the conversation of his fellow collegiates', one of whom, described as 'a morose and importunate Master of Arts', drove him out of college by noisily playing indoor bowls in the room below him. I happen to know this set of rooms, and can witness that its parallel half-timbered walls make it something like a bowling alley. It is known in college as Cow Lane, because someone once let a cow into it, as if in a stall. Be that as it may, all this, which might sound like the petty squabbling and anecdotage of a closed academic society, is told with such enjoyment, good humour, and sympathy that Roger North's life of his brother may well stand as the first intimate biography in English.

Intimate biography brings us, of course, to Johnson and Boswell. So much has been written about this first great, and perhaps still the greatest biography, that one need perhaps only indicate features that are sometimes forgotten. First Boswell on Johnson is, among everything else, a biographer on a biographer. Samuel Johnson, in his *Lives of the Poets*, still more in his substantial life of Richard Savage, had shown himself a great writer of life-studies. His life of Savage is unique for its time, in that it is not only the life of a very unsuccessful man, but of one who was in many respects a scoundrel. Biography, which had begun as the laudation of a noble life, was for the first time stood on its head. Life itself is what interests Johnson, and what he assumes will interest us. True, he accepts Savage's personal history somewhat at Savage's own valuation, his hints of noble illegitimacy and all; but he does not minimize the extent to which he was an importunate borrower, a frequent swindler, and professionally vain; all this with sympathy, even for the egregious Savage's boasting as an author. In Johnson's words,

> *He could not easily leave off when he had begun to mention himself or his works: nor ever read his verses without stealing his eye from the page to discover in*

the faces of his audience how they were affected by any favourite passage.

Boswell, then, in writing about Johnson after his death, had, so to speak, to live up to, and surpass, the biographies Johnson himself had written during life. He even outdid Johnson in thoroughness. To take only one example among many, he constructed his scene of the interview between Johnson and George III from at least half-a-dozen sources. Then again, the popular idea that Boswell's *Life* simply consists of his noting down the fine things said by Johnson, that all its virtue lies in it being Johnson's own words, leaves out of account how much genuine original research went into it. Johnson was 54 when Boswell met him. The care and scholarship Boswell, with his logical, legal mind, expended on those fifty-four years, has always been underestimated. The account is so full and convincing that one forgets the numerical disproportion of the whole book, one-fifth on these years, four-fifths on the remaining twenty of Johnson's life. Boswell, perhaps stimulated by the erroneous attempt at a Life by Sir John Hawkins, Johnson's executor but no biographer, took exceptional pains to write Johnson's early history so that the same man, with the same characteristic nature, appears throughout. It is a wonderful feat of assimilation. Finally, as only the publication of Boswell's own journals has proved, Boswell was himself a consummate writer. His prose stands up to Johnson's own, whereas Hawkins's, in the account mentioned, was so stiff and inflexible as to invite the contemporary parody it received at the hands of the dramatist, Arthur Murphy. Boswell's *Johnson* combines scientific, scholarly research with the artist's use of words. It is what we mean today by biography. No isolated quotation can do it justice, but scene after scene lives as if we had seen or heard it upon a stage – Wilkes, the arch-enemy, mollifying Johnson by helping him to the best cuts of roast veal: 'A little of the brown, sir – Some fat, sir – a little of the stuffing – Some gravy? Let me have the pleasure of giving you some butter – Allow me to recommend a squeeze of this orange – or this lemon perhaps may have more zest,' and so on. Boswell's legal accuracy, real affection, drama, utter frankness, and, for all the fun, genuine seriousness, produced a masterpiece.

However, as if to prove once again how fragile is the myth of inevitable progress, the nineteenth century produced no biography comparable with Boswell's, and the process of biography in English itself suffered a severe setback. This was almost entirely due to the Evangelical movement and its hold on the emerging middle classes. The Evangelical doctrine of salvation, and the exclusiveness of those saved, laid tremendous, and to us now frightening stress on conduct to maintain that state. No amusement, no relaxation, no light or trivial reading in particular, was permitted. The word 'serious' prevailed; well-to-do people even advertised for a 'serious' footman, butler, or housekeeper. The definition of 'serious reading' was stringent. Boswell himself would certainly not have passed the test. Every word must be improving. Mudie's Circulating Library, W. H. Smith's chain of bookshops, and at juvenile level *The Boy's Own Paper* were founded by Evangelicals to provide and circulate 'good' literature. Pockets of orthodox Evangelicalism exist to this day, households where a radio or television set has never been known. In the last decade of the nineteenth century, an Evangelical bishop used his influence with W. H. Smith's railway bookshops to ban every novel by that immoral author of *Tess of the d'Urbervilles* and of *Jude the Obscure*, Thomas Hardy; in a recent pornographic book trial, it transpired that the telephoned code message 'W. H. Smith' meant 'The police are coming. Display only decent books in your window.' The effect on biography, still more on biographers, was disastrous. The biographer's heroes and heroines could do no wrong; any that they did was swept under the carpet. Thus the poet laureate, Robert Southey, in his life of Nelson, had to say, of the great hero-admiral's notorious affair with Lady Hamilton,

There is no reason to believe that this most unfortunate attachment was criminal [i.e. sexual], but this was

criminality enough, and it brought with it its punishment.

Biography became, in part, the art of concealment. Illegitimate children do not exist; so Emma Hamilton's own feelings for Nelson in Southey's words, 'did not, in reality, pass the bounds of ardent and romantic admiration'. This type of biography, written not to reveal but to conceal human nature, persisted throughout the century. Forster's life of Dickens not only conceals the novelist's estrangement from his wife and his shifts to meet his mistress Ellen Ternan; it blankets Dickens's manic-depressive character, his half-mad outbursts of insult and anger, anything that deviates from the popular picture of a great, spiritually inspiring, and above all Christian writer. Besides, biographers often had their eye on the great man's widow – or even worse, were the widow.

Three Victorian biographers only broke out of this paralysing moral strait-jacket. Carlyle, with his slogan from his own essay on Boswell, 'History is the new poetry', wrote what were virtually long, dithyrambic, biographical prose-poems. With his constant personal interpolations in this vein – 'Heavens, human language is unequal to the history of such things', he exclaims at one point, though the spate of words that follows belies such modesty – his life of Frederick the Great has its counterpart in the long dramatic poems of Browning rather than any type of biography. There is even an exact parallel between his blonde vanished women of the Prussian Court and those

> *Dear, dead women with such hair too – what became of all the gold?*

in Browning's *A Toccata of Galuppi's*. Yet if Carlyle evaded in pseudo-poetry the issues of biography, Mrs Gaskell with her admirable *Charlotte Brontë* met them head on, in what is arguably the best English biography of the nineteenth century. She had advantages which set her apart from her contemporaries. A Unitarian, and wife of an Unitarian minister, the intellectual aristocracy of English nonconformists, she had no use for Evangelical piety. The school of the Reverend Carus Wilson, which killed two of Charlotte's sisters, and half-ruined Charlotte's own life, was not to be exempted from critical scrutiny because it was run on sound Evangelical principles. Though she had to treat the feelings of Charlotte's bereaved father and widowed husband with tact, she could not produce a life to satisfy, in a misty rhetoric of piety, these two possessive clergymen. Charlotte emerges as a real smouldering person, a credible creator of the barely-concealed and sometimes quite unconcealed passions of *Jane Eyre* and *Villette*. Finally, the biographer of Carlyle, J. A. Froude, tried to show, from the papers handed to him by Carlyle himself, what Carlyle was really like. Handicapped by confusing instructions – one day Carlyle wanted all told, the next nearly all concealed – Froude did a fairly faithful job, only to be execrated for his pains by Alfred, Lord Tennyson, among others.

This general regression had two interesting results for our present century. One was that the numerous pious lives of heroes and heroines, suitable for prizes, short ones for children at Sunday School, extremely long ones for university or theological students, three-volume monsters for family reading by father, all left the real life virtually untouched and unexplored. Some of the best twentieth-century biographies owe their startling originality to the masking effect of the pious official life. Dorothy Pattison, the Florence Nightingale of the factory worker, had a popular Victorian biography stressing her happy family background and exemplary life as an Anglican nun. In fact, though herself a sincere religious, her family upbringing was so horrific as to make the home life of the Brontës seem by comparison like a quiet tea-party, and her novice's habit did not prevent her from falling in love with handsome men literally to the end of her days. Secondly, the reaction, when it came, was both violent and ignorant, particularly in the hands of that self-contradictory figure, Lytton Strachey.

As a biographer, Strachey is the classic example of doing the right things for the wrong reason. He thought and said that most Victorian biography was longwinded humbug. He said this so well that one must quote from his introduction to *Eminent Victorians*.

He writes of

> *those two fat volumes with which it is our custom to*
> *commemorate the dead – who does not know them, with*
> *their ill-digested masses of material, their slipshod*
> *style, their tone of tedious panegyric, their lamentable*
> *lack of selection, of detachment, of design? They are*
> *as familiar as the cortege of the undertaker and wear*
> *the same air of slow, funereal barbarism.*

One must also add, as typical of Strachey, that this
whole passage, the image of the undertaker included,
was stolen, unacknowledged, from a passage by
Edmund Gosse, written seventeen years earlier, and
beginning, 'We in England bury our dead under the
monstrous catafalque of two volumes (crown octavo).'
In fact, never understanding the Victorians, about
whom he wrote so wittily, Strachey mistook the
natural length of Victorian family reading, two or
three volumes, for deliberate padding, and the language perfectly natural to Evangelical works, with its
Biblical reference, for insincerity and hypocrisy. His
own Bloomsbury style was just as insincere and hypocritical in its own way, with references to psycho-
analysis and sex substituted for God and religion. He
accused Victorian biographers of suppression but
himself suppressed every bit of historical evidence that
did not make a 'good', this time in the sense of
'scandalous', story. It is doubtful whether he ever

read one truly first-hand source. His best-known stories, such as that of General Gordon retiring to his tent with a Bible and brandy-bottle, and emerging, many hours later, visibly much more inspired by the brandy-bottle, derive from third-hand printed sources and dubious ones at that. Yet he brought back to biography what it had lost since Boswell. He was excited by man's real nature, and he was supremely readable. After Strachey, no good biographer has dared to be less than an artist. Biography designed as literature derives mainly from him.

The biographers of the past fifty years since Strachey's last work are those from whose efforts, from whose experience and my own, I shall illustrate the actual practising methods of English biography as it appears today. These fifty years have been a golden age of biography. At no other time in the world's history have so many and so fine biographical studies been written or so well received by the public. On the shelves of our libraries, public and private, hardback and paperback, in our bookstores, academic or general, biography of every sort, literary, historical, or scientific, fills almost the longest footage. In addition, there is now even a journal devoted to studies in biography.

It would seem that biography, first looking on man as an adjunct to religious example and precept of moral conduct, a part of the prevailing Church, then as an ornament to the prevailing State, an example of civic, secular virtues, has gradually come to portray as its subject the individual man or woman. It has been a movement towards humanism, and may take its place, and account for its own popularity, as a humanistic study. It has also developed from the official to the unofficial; it has admitted the lesser known, in their capacity and interest simply as human beings. This is modern biography. How it achieves its undoubted, general success and interest, by what methods, artistic and scientific, I now hope to trace.

2
Present Practice

Lytton Strachey's *Eminent Victorians* appeared nearly sixty years ago. Such was the power of Strachey's style, the sheer literary virtuosity, that it is often said to have set the tone for the practice of modern biography. Yet, as I have suggested, Strachey did little more than substitute one set of accepted symbols for another. His biographies are very much of their time and for their time. They embody the cynicism of the years after the gigantic slaughter of the 1914–18 war. Then again, it is often said that Strachey introduced into biography the methods of Freudian analysis. Since Freud's *General Introduction to Psycho-Analysis* did not appear in English translation until two years after *Eminent Victorians*, this seems unlikely, even though the translator was Strachey's brother. What Strachey introduced was more the biography of psychological innuendo. For example, in his *Florence Nightingale*, he asks

Why, as a child in the nursery, when her sister had
shown a healthy pleasure in tearing her dolls to pieces,
had she *shown an almost morbid one in sewing them*
up again?

The amateur psychology of this sentence is laughable,
in its assumption that it is 'healthy' – i.e. unrepressed –
to tear dolls to pieces (there is no evidence that
Florence's sister did), and 'morbid' – i.e. repressed –
to mend them.

Strachey's approach to his characters might better
be called humanistic and rationalizing rather than
analytical. No one would deny, though, that psycho-
analysis and the exploration of the unconscious has
given a new skill for the modern biographer to use.
We do not write as we might have done before Freud.
Yet the most valuable function of this weapon of
awareness in the biographer's armoury is that he
examines more carefully the motives not of his
characters, but of his own self while writing. This
self-analysis has made us, if not better biographers,
certainly more honest ones. We cannot indulge, even
if we wanted to, in the sweeping cynicism of a Strachey
on Florence Nightingale, nor in the pious camouflage
of a Forster on Dickens, without questioning deeply
our own fitness for such judgements, and our own
motives in making them. The first method of modern
biography is this self-analysis. One of its virtues is the
humane approach to the idiosyncrasies and apparent

contradictions of our subject. Only by submitting ourselves to this somewhat searching process, and continuing to do so while writing and studying, can we be alert to the unconscious in the men or women we are writing about.

Simple psycho-analytical biography, however, which applies the formulae of a known practitioner, a Freud or a Jung, to the evidence about a subject's life, has had very few successes. 'A Man's life of any worth', to quote Keats, defies such simplification, except at the risk of misrepresentation. Two such modern lives of Keats, in fact, spring to mind, one Freudian, one Jungian. Both, though useful and interesting, seem flawed by this tendency to misrepresent the evidence, often in the most obvious way, at points where it does not accord with psycho-analytical theory. Both, in this attempt, quote Keats's actual poems, and interpret passages from them, in a way that indicates either an obstinate carelessness in the reading, or an actual misreading, making Keats use words which the poem does not contain.

To take first the Freudian approach. Keats, as is well known, lost his mother when he was only thirteen. She died in circumstances which were particularly poignant for him. She was at that time his sole parent, the father having been killed in an accident some years before. An eldest son, Keats was specially attached to his mother, and she to him, though she had led an irregular life, and absented herself from her children for long periods. The tuberculosis which had already carried off her own two brothers now attacked her, still only in her thirties and an attractive woman. Keats was on holiday from the small residential school he attended. He devoted this holiday to nursing his mother. He read her books, he told her stories, he mixed and administered the useless medicines she had been prescribed, with constant faith that he could help her to recover. The shock of death, when he heard it next term at school, was devastating. His school-fellows write of a complete though temporary collapse. Naturally, Freudian interpretation has found extreme signs of mother-fixation in the poems he later began to write, especially his earlier poems nearer the event, and, less technically skilled than his mature work, more open to treatment as documents of his personal unconscious.

One of these is the long, rambling unfinished poem, which Keats himself referred to as his 'Endymion', although it was in fact an episodic and disorganized dress-rehearsal for the famous, later finished poem of that name. This earlier poem, just before it breaks off, has a strange passage where Keats imagines the bridal night of Endymion and his Cynthia, goddess of the Moon, as having a mystic effect on the inhabitants of this earth. The world is filled with universal lovemaking, its healthy inhabitants seem to take on immortal strength and beauty, while the long-despaired-of sufferers from illness are shown as suddenly and

44

miraculously cured before the eyes of their wondering families.

The languid sick: it cooled their fevered sleep,
And soothed them into slumbers full and deep.
Soon they awoke clear eyed: nor burnt with thirsting,
Nor with hot fingers, nor with temples bursting:
And springing up, they met the wondering sight
Of their dear friends, near foolish with delight.

To the Freudian biographer, this is a passage about Keats's mother. It is a description of a wish-fulfilment state, in which all that the adolescent Keats had dreamt might be possible, his mother's recovery, is relived in fantasy. Yet 'the languid sick', with whom the passage begins and ends, are everywhere not singular but plural. There is no picture that suggests a dying woman. Viewed in the context of Keats's life when he was composing it, the passage coincides with his decision to throw up his hospital work as a qualified doctor, and to serve mankind instead by the craft of poetry rather than by that of surgery. 'The languid sick' were those he had seen in their thousands, in the wards of Guy's Hospital, and worked to cure, not the image of a mother-fixated man still in fancy at the death-bed of one woman to which a psycho-analytic approach confines it. In fact, medical experience had made Keats grow up and mature far beyond such adolescent fixation.

If a Freudian prejudice about this passage has led the writer to a most unlikely biographical judgement, a Jungian prejudice about another Keats poem has led a writer actually to misread its text. The poem is *La Belle Dame Sans Merci*, and the passage given a Jungian significance is the Knight-at-Arms'

And there I shut her wild, wild eyes
With kisses four.

on which Keats joked that he had to make it an even number for each eye. Certainly the lines seem plain enough, in the sense that they say who is doing what, and to whom. It is the Knight who kisses the lady four times – 'And there *I* shut her wild, wild eyes, with kisses four'. In the effort to pin a meaning on La Belle Dame herself, however, a Jungian biographer has pounced on the Jungian concept that Four is the number which represents the archetypal Self. The Knight-at-Arms, interpreted here as the poet, is represented as in thrall to the Self, and the choice of four kisses as significant. To the astonishment, it must seem, of any reader who has studied this very well-known poem even superficially, it appears that the Jungian biographer has misread these lines themselves. The biography, to set the Jungian record right, specifically speaks of 'La Belle Dame kissing her knight precisely four times', and states that Keats, though puzzled, was led by his Jungian Unconscious

46

to choose this number for La Belle Dame or Self to employ. Yet this, of course, is a total misreading. The Knight kisses the Lady, not the Lady the Knight. A preconceived psycho-analytical idea has caused a biographer, acute in other ways, completely to reverse a familiar quotation.

This is not to deny the great benefits of psychoanalytic approaches in heightening our awareness of human nature and its possible interpretations. Yet most attempts to fit a biography to the procrustean bed of one or other of the main psycho-analytical systems have failed because of their preconceived rigidity of doctrine. Only in exceptional cases, such as Ernest Jones's own biography of Freud himself, do they seem to be appropriate. They are, as these examples suggest, particularly misleading in literary biography, when joined with the dangerous pastime of reading an artist's creative fictions as guides to the events of his or her life. Yet there are notable successes even here. One of the best is the biography by Peter Green of Kenneth Grahame, author of *The Wind in the Willows*. Green touches on this book as an unconscious idyll of the author's homosexual longings. It is an ideal life of little furry bachelor animals, all male, and delighting in each other's friendship. Green goes further than this, and makes the work illustrate a social and historical event in England. This is the trial, in 1895, of Oscar Wilde. The prison sentence on Wilde had a double effect on English homosexuals. Alarmed by the threat

47

of punitive police activity, many fled abroad; others felt able to protect themselves by accepting a heterosexual and outwardly conformist marriage. Among these was probably Grahame, who married a minor verse-writer, Elspeth Thomson. For Grahame his previous existence became 'A Golden Age', the actual title of one of his other books, ostensibly about childhood. Looking back, some years later, he produced his classic *The Wind in the Willows*. This does more than reproduce, in a disguised animal world, idyllic bachelor freedom. It introduces a loveable but potentially disruptive character, whose adventures become the mainspring of the plot. This is Toad, whom the biographer, with great acuteness, has seen as Grahame's hero in a sub-conscious projection of the drama of Oscar Wilde. Boastful, vain, addicted to fancy waistcoats and extravagant poses, Toad has characteristics which are, almost word for word, those of Wilde. When arrested and brought before the magistrate, he cannot resist insulting that official with would-be witty remarks, 'quantities of imaginative cheek', exactly as Wilde behaved to his judge. His sentence is said to be harsher because of his behaviour in the witness-box, as it undoubtedly was with Wilde. The comic horror of his pursuit by 'policemen with truncheons' is the dread felt by many homosexuals at the time that police action of a violent kind would be unleashed on them, and their need to flee, even to leave the country. Toad finally even composes a ballad on his experiences, as

Wilde wrote 'The Ballad of Reading Gaol'. The biographer's exploration of Grahame's subconscious has produced a notable connection between his subject's life and the social history of the time.

One of the chief innovations of modern biography, then, is the use it makes of evidence about the psychic, subconscious life of its subject. More exact medical science of the past 175 years has brought a wealth of possible and relevant evidence about the physical state of the subject of biography. One must always heed Tolstoi's warning here, that the state of health can be a fallible guide: Napoleon did not lose the battle of Borodino simply because he had a cold in the head. Yet since perhaps the distinguishing mark of modern biography over what has gone before, that it aims to take account of every aspect of a man or woman's life, conscious or unconscious, psychic or physical, public or private, physical states, especially long-term or deeply-laid, must be important to the biographer, medical death certificates attesting cause of death, and signed by a qualified medical practitioner, introduced in England 140 years ago, have become a prime source of evidence, which the better minimal medical education initiated by the Apothecaries Act of 1815 has made valuable and valid. Such a death certificate has recently thrown light on a vital aspect of the life and work of Thomas Hardy. Hardy, as is well known, wrote dozens of his finest poems to the memory of his dead first wife. So astonishing is the quality of this work that some critics have preferred it to anything else written by him, and have naturally tried to enquire for causes of this quality. Hardy has added to the biographical puzzle by saying that these remarkable poems formed what he called 'an expiation'. The poems indeed are loaded with the poet's guilt. However, when they speak of the nature of this guilt, the causes they give seem extraordinarily trivial. Hardy, it seems from his own evidence, was inconsiderate to his wife in a number of minor ways. He did not take her on holidays to her favourite resorts, he failed latterly to respond to her singing at the piano, he was taciturn to her, and lacking in domestic conversation. He writes of this, quite specifically.

Why then, latterly, did we not speak,
Did we not think of those days long dead,
And ere your vanishing strive to seek
That time's renewal? We might have said,
'In this bright spring weather
We'll visit together
Those places that once we visited'

These omissions are what many husbands might reproach themselves with, but hardly to the extent of inspiring 'an expiation' of some hundred deeply moving poems. One's suspicions that there was more to expiate might well be aroused by one circumstance. Hardy insisted, to an unnatural degree, how unexpected his wife's death was. She seemed perfectly healthy, he continually insists on saying, right up to the day before her death. Casual evidence, however, accumulated over the years, seems to deny this. Eye-witness accounts speak of her being in such pain that she was weeping before visitors. A letter has emerged revealing that she could not walk the short distance to the local church, where she was a devout worshipper, but had to be wheeled by the gardener in a bathchair. A special maidservant was engaged at the Hardy home, whose main duty, it now transpires from an interview with the actual woman, was to massage Mrs Hardy to relieve a somewhat mysterious but acute pain from which she suffered. Her death certificate reveals that far from dying from a sudden heart-attack, which would accord with Hardy's own story of the un-expectedness of her death, her prime cause of death, attested by the family doctor, was impacted gallstones. This condition would have caused intense pain over a long period, be consistent with her weakness and in-ability to walk, and bring about referred pains which the maid's massage might temporarily assuage. Hardy must have known, for some time, of his wife's agoniz-ing sufferings, but for various reasons chose to ignore them, and even to pretend that they had not existed. When the enormity of this conduct was brought home to him by her death, he therefore had not mere minor, commonplace marital inconsiderations with which to reproach himself, but an indifference to a suffering human being and an actual physical neglect which amounted virtually to a crime. His use of the word 'expiation' was no exaggeration. The deeply felt remorse and self-horror of the poems becomes for the first time explicable in simple, physical terms alone, while one's whole view of Hardy as a man is also affected.

Medical science can be used by the modern biographer to determine physical states in the subject of biography, which may have far-reaching historical consequences. A popular recent use has been the investigation into the 'madness' of George III. Heeding Tolstoi's warning about Napoleon's cold and the Battle of Borodino, one cannot of course say that the events of 1776 were in consequence of the erratic behaviour of the King of England. At the same time, that behaviour must be worth the study of the biographer. The theory of Dr Richard Hunter is that the King should not be considered 'mad' but the victim of a hereditary metabolic defect. George III, it appears, was not in the grip of insanity as such, but suffered periodic attacks of a rare blood condition, porphyria, which, by its effect on the blood-stream, causes mental confusion in a way entirely consistent with the documentary evidence and the dating of his apparent mania. The results of this make his judgement, or lack of judgement, in politics fully explicable in biography for the first time.

This kind of biographical study, sometimes alarming

in its implications, has been well demonstrated in a work written during the last decade, *The Pathology of Leadership* by Dr Hugh L'Etang. It is alarming along the lines of Dean Rusk's picture, quoted by Dr L'Etang, of the global affairs of nations depending on the discussions of two heads of state, one with high blood pressure, the other with 'a quick temper and a weak heart'. L'Etang's brief biographies of twentieth-century political leaders are, of course, as he admits, biased by being too exclusively medical in their use of evidence. At the same time they indicate the usefulness of medical evidence for biography. Early in the 1940s, at a delicate point in Anglo-American relations over war-aid, a British Ambassador startled American newsmen, on his arrival in the United States at a crucial point in negotiations, by announcing, 'Well, boys, Britain's broke. It's your money we want.' Incredulity, which also included blame for those in Britain who had sent him on this mission, was only assuaged by the knowledge, which emerged years later, that he was in fact suffering from an acute kidney disease, putting him in a state of stupor, in which he literally cannot have known what he was saying. It also seems, from Dr L'Etang's scientific analysis, that modern biographers should know not only what diseases their subjects are suffering but who their doctors were, and what curative or palliative drugs these doctors were likely to have been prescribing: in other words, that the biographer's research must extend not only to a person's own life but to the life of his physician.

This examination of physical evidence has made the modern biographer's task more exacting. He or she must interpret medical and scientific language, which is constantly changing, as the science itself alters. The biographer has to interpret, for example, early and more imprecise medical terms. One learns that whereas death by what is called in parish registers 'a decline' probably means pulmonary tuberculosis, death by what is called 'a deep decline' probably means tuberculous meningitis. The biographer of the whole life must also give a convincing account of the final issue of all life-studies, death itself. Many conventional biographers evade this description, either by a laconic brevity, or by a deliberate piece of fine writing. Accounts of Keats's prolonged death agonies, denied the laudanum which he himself had purchased in order deliberately to end his life, are muffled by the well-meaning and over-sympathetic biographer, who produces instead fine prose passages about the beauties of the Roman Spring.

Perhaps even more important to a modern biographer than study of the psychological or medical background is the full appreciation of economic and social circumstances. If Freud was not such a powerful influence on biography as we may have thought, Marx most certainly has been. We no longer see any man and woman in isolation, divorced from his or her class and economic situation, from the whole social structure of the world during their life-spans. The lives of so many nineteenth-century notables can now be seen as part of a class-struggle, a struggle in which even the supreme genius of a Dickens or a Thomas Hardy might receive both inspiration but also damage. An instructive example is the sequence of biographies about that key nineteenth-century English figure, William Morris.

Morris came to socialism partly through his revolt, as a craftsman, against the shoddy materialism that had evolved from the worst features of the Industrial Revolution. He lived and worked in continual protest against the shallow self-interest of the Victorian middle-class from which he himself sprang. His first biographer, whose work appeared in the year 1899, would seem to have unique qualifications and advantages for such a study. This man, J. W. Mackail, was an Oxford scholar of great literary gifts: he had won the Newdigate poetry prize at that university, and taken every conceivable academic honour. He was the son-in-law of Edward Burne-Jones, Morris's lifelong friend and working partner. He had the confidences and help of Lady Burne-Jones, with whom Morris had been hopelessly in love. He had letters, documents, business and confidential matter, access to intimate conversation, first-hand evidence which would be a modern biographer's dream. One must, of course, make allowance for standard Victorian reticence.

There were some of Morris's private matters which, Mackail himself said, one would have inserted in the book 'if,' as he put it, 'one were going to die the day before it was published'. Yet Mackail's biography fails to be more than a skilful, artistic compilation of this rough, working material for one absolutely vital reason. He never, or hardly ever, attempts to set what Morris was aiming to do against the economic, social, and political movements and conditions of Morris's own times. In fact, Mackail explicitly rejects any idea of doing so. Faced with Morris, who after all studied Marx closely if with effort, and the problems he found in early English Socialism, Mackail writes:

A biographer would be straying far beyond the limits of his appointed task if he became the analyst of social conditions or a historian of institutions.

Mackail therefore makes no attempt to show how and why socialism, and the rise of the Christian Socialist movement in England, held such an appeal for Morris, and seemed a justification of all his work. In fact, he even treats Socialism as something of an aberration for Morris, a by-way of his artistic concerns, instead of seeing the artist as inspired by the new Socialistic movement and philosophy, and wholly a part of it in all he did. No less than three modern biographies, in the last twenty years, have redressed the balance. By contrast, they perhaps stress too insistently Morris's involvement with socialism; but they see him not as an isolated individual, but one with the progress of the movement from vague Ruskinian socialism, through Christian Socialism to the political socialism of the London Marxists and the early Bernard Shaw.

Not only economic and social movements but the events of political history must now be the province of the biographer. One of the most fascinating biographies in this respect is Harold Nicolson's life of King George the Fifth. What could have been a dull and conventionally respectful portrait of royalty is made living and important by the author's realization of the political, social, and economic problems facing the King in the dramatic quarter-century of his rule. Nicolson, himself a middle-rank politician, places the King, an ordinary simple man, who had no wish to come to the throne, against the most horrific political turmoil and social change that any British monarch has ever experienced. From the beginning, this straight-forward, honest-minded naval officer faced continuous crisis on huge issues – a constitutional crisis at the start, then the First World War of global proportions, the emergence of Parliamentary Labour, the general strike, the massive economic depression of the early 1930s, the collapse of the hopes for world peace, and, in his last years, the seemingly inevitable rise of the European dictators. Against the full background of these cataclysmic events, the biographer shows us an ordinary, not specially gifted, but honest man of common sense, who happened to be born in a royal family, often puzzled, not infrequently irritated, never merely stupid, a plain man with simple reactions of basic decency. Difficult as this may have been for his ministers, who had, for instance, to persuade him to meet Soviet representatives, whom he regarded, not altogether unjustly, as murderers of his Russian cousin, the Czar, the King's common humanity in the political welter of self-interest and ambition is an epic of biography. Nicolson, by giving full value and understanding to all the political movements of the King's reign, has produced a portrait enhanced, not diminished, by this large-scale background of events. Nicolson, as a politician himself, impotent to influence events, brings a deep sympathetic understanding of the King.

The new biography demands that the biographer should suffer, realistically if vicariously, with the sufferings of his subject. W. H. Auden wrote that the novelist

In his own weak person, if he can,
Must suffer dully all the wrongs of Man.

The biographer must suffer, not dully but acutely, not only the wrongs but all the experiences, triumphant or disastrous, of the subject whose life he attempts to recreate.

This raises the large problem of the writer's

identification with his subject, which can lead equally to the triumphs or disasters of biography itself. There is surely no guide to whether one's identification with the subject is too much or too little; it is a matter of the most subtle gradations, of which the conscientious biographer must be continually and actively aware. One advantage has certainly come with our age of greater mobility and travel. A biographer can, geographically and literally, put himself in the footsteps of his subject. Less exacting and perhaps less profound than entering into the mental states of the subject, it is at any rate more likely to be accurate, and can bring some of the highest successes to the biographer. The classic example in our century is G. M. Trevelyan in his great three-volume biography of Garibaldi. Trevelyan, an indefatigable pedestrian, with long, gaunt, raking steps and unquenchable energy, actually walked, often in the heat of the south Italian sun, over every yard of Italian soil that Garibaldi and his armies had covered. If hard-pressed for time, he occasionally mounted a bicycle, though not often. The result is a *tour de force* of identification, shared by the reader, which could not have been achieved in any other way. Trevelyan lay on the stony Sicilian hillside at Calatafimi, where Garibaldi's handful of liberating troops were exposed to the fire of the Austrians encamped higher up. He experienced their thirst, isolation, exposure. He also could imaginatively experience, thanks to this exercise, the moment, one of the greatest in his biography, when a heavy stone lands on Garibaldi's back. By inspired mistake, or bluff, the Italian leader persuades his men that, out of ammunition, the Austrians are reduced to throwing stones as missiles, and he orders an uphill charge which sweeps the enemy off the summit. It is one of the finest intimate reconstructions in all biography, with its details of the heat, the rough hill-surface, the aromatic scent of herbs and flowers, experienced by the biographer in his own person.

Personal use of all the senses, personal experience of all places described, now seems essential for the biographer. This is not to deny the remarkable feats performed without such means. The American biographer, William Hickling Prescott, though, as is well known, virtually blind, achieved the most amazing reconstruction of the landscape and civilization of Spanish America, which he was denied the ability ever to see. Generally speaking, however, a biographer's experience not only of place, but of climate and time also, is invaluable. The later stages of Keats's *Endymion* were composed while he was staying at the foot of Box Hill near Dorking, some twenty-five miles south-west of London, in the later part of November 1817. In these lines, he makes Endymion plan an ideal landscape in which to live.

> *Where shall our dwelling be? Under the brow*
> *Of some steep mossy hill, where ivy dun*

Would hide us up, although spring leaves were none;
And where dark yew-trees, as we rustle through,
Will drop their scarlet berry-cups of dew? . . .
For by one step the blue sky shouldst thou find,
And by another, in deep dell below,
See through its trees a little river go
All in its mid-day gold and glimmering.

If one visits this place in the last week in November, when Keats wrote those lines, one can literally follow the footsteps of the poet and see how he translates physical facts into his hero's fictional landscape. The hill rises immediately and steeply, with mossy slopes and dark trails of ivy. About fifty yards above Keats's starting-place, it divides into two paths. The track straight up the hill narrows and leads one to climb upward flanked closely by yew bushes, whose scarlet fruit, at that time of the year and at no other, are so soft and ripe that as one, like the poet's hero, 'rustles through', they patter down at one's feet. Straight ahead is the cold, blue November sky at the hill-top. If one turns aside, to follow the second path to the right, it leads along a sharp edge. The 'deep dell' of the poem drops westward away so that one hangs over a 'little river', again with the poet, which exactly at 'mid-day', as in the poem, catches the sun which, coming over the eastern brow of the hill, sheds on it a gleam of wintry sunshine: 'All in its mid-day gold and glimmering.' The poet has described in his heroic poem his own mid-day paths. We, taking that journey, at exactly the same time of year, and only then, when all the events of this part of the poem occur, imaginatively relive every detail of the poet's inspiration some 160 years ago, and take part in these incidents of his personal life.

More arduously than taking part in the physical and outward life of our subject, we must try to take part in his or her inward and spiritual life. This now makes great demands on sympathy and understanding; yet without it, the study of many figures in history, great and small, would be meaningless. Whole areas, particularly in the seventeenth and nineteenth century, need to be explored for this inner life. One is not talking solely about the religious mystics, whose exact belief is perhaps impenetrable, but more especially of those who expressed their belief in action, a William Penn or an Oliver Cromwell, a Wilberforce or a Shaftesbury. We must see that the words themselves, in which they expressed their beliefs, are not far-fetched, exaggerated, and certainly not hypocritical – Strachey's mistake – but a language natural to the inward light by which they lived, and which they held in common with a great many other believers of their time. We must abandon our own age, in which such expressions might indicate insincerity, and take them at their own sincere face-value. To understand feelingly another person's religion and spiritual life across the ages is perhaps the biographer's most difficult task.

The biographer has a duty to be neither dismissive nor dogmatic, sympathetic even where one cannot oneself completely follow.

All these skills – psychological, medical, economic, political, geographical, religious – are now part of the equipment of the modern biographer. All these arts and sciences may at any time be demanded by the biography of any subject, leaving out of account any special skills needed for the particular profession of the subject: for example, an appreciation of painting, for a painter, of military science and history for a general. How can any one biographer master and employ these skills? That he or she can do so appears by the many comprehensive, well-informed, and factually accurate lives that appear almost every day. One answer to the problem raised by the sheer bulk of evidence has, of course, been provided by the simple, physical aids to the mass of scattered documentation: the photocopier, the microfilms, the sophisticated facilities of most modern libraries and collections. The researcher is no longer in the position of the legal adviser, employed about a hundred years ago, to study the Chancery records which involved the inheritance that should have come to Keats. This worthy gentleman complained that on a dark, foggy, Victorian London day, the light in the Public Record Office, Chancery Lane, became so bad that he had frequently to give up work. That this happened within living memory is vouched for by older attendants at the office, who speak of a tradition – now mercifully a thing of the past – that researchers should be handicapped as much as possible so that, when all had gone prematurely away, the staff could settle down and play cards by Government-provided candlelight. That bizarre but well-attested story could happen nowhere today, and the biographer, surrounded by photocopy and micro-film, may produce the most exotic life, charting the voyages of Captain Cook, or the course of a global warleader, without ever leaving his own home town. Yet such facilities, while meeting the new complexities of the subject, bring their own dangers. Though we saw that Strachey's claim to initiate a new type of biography was exaggerated, it contained one element which the well-provided modern biographer would do well to heed. This is Strachey's insistence on style and brevity, on artistic choice and unity, biography as an artistic whole. Strachey, to give him the credit which may seem to have been grudged earlier, waged a successful campaign for the biography of artistic selection against the rag-bag life-and-times monsters of nineteenth-century biography. He headed a long line of writers – David Cecil, Harold Nicolson, Cecil Woodham-Smith, to name only a few – who have produced miniature but satisfying masterpieces. Yet, in the enthusiasm for the comprehensive use of all available evidence, modern biography has shown an opposite tendency. The monster has crept back, in the ugly guise of the so-called 'definitive' life, the record which is meant to surpass in sheer completeness all other records, past or possible future.

It is just here that the modern biographer needs most the saving grace of proportion and, perhaps the best gift to any life-study, ordinary common sense. Simple arithmetic, commonplace as such a gift may sound, is surely a necessary equipment for anyone considering any subject for biographical study. It is clear by some modern examples that this has not always been applied. To take one area of biography alone, the Romantic poets were prolific of biographical evidence. Supremely interested in the working of their own psyches, they provided almost a case-book of their development, of which the letters of Keats, to take only one example, but that a supreme one, bear full witness. Yet does his brief though packed life, however fully documented, thanks largely to its great specialized collection in the Houghton Library at Harvard, yet a mere twenty-five years life-span, honestly justify a biography of nearly half a million words? The record on Byron is huge, his extra-poetic activities, lurid and otherwise, immense: yet does that life, again relatively brief, honestly justify the expenditure of close on one million words? Wordsworth we know, lived his full eighty years. Yet, apart from his tempestuous, revolutionary youth, it was a life of singularly little incident. How have his biographers managed to approach one million words on *him*? If, as Browning reminded us, we hardly need to know 'what porridge had John

Keats', do we really need to know what meals the faithful Dorothy Wordsworth cooked for her William? Perhaps these numerical cavils may seem trivial: but it is healthy to remind ourselves that the sheer weight of evidence now available to a biographer does not in itself make a successful biography.

One would not, of course, wish to check too positively such passion for detail, which can often provide, out of smallest means, the largest insights. Yet one suspects that a good deal of this excessive length in biography too often comes not from a passion for detail, but from a passion for controversy and for self-justification. Too often, the text of the book is lengthened, to the ordinary reader's dismay, by arguments with other scholars and earlier biographers. Such private, professional controversy seldom helps the reader, and may greatly hinder the narrative. It has a most valuable place, in some instances, but that place is surely in the footnotes, or, in extreme cases, as when some erroneous legend has taken specially obstinate hold, in a separate appendix. This is the way one would have it, and most biographers now follow some such methods. Yet too often the passion for crossing swords in public brings purely academic argument in the text, to the discomfort of the reader. There is one very long biography of Robert Browning where, in spite of argument being placed in footnote and appendix, it is duplicated by being retained in the text as well. Even the names of the academic authorities to be controverted appear among the historic characters of the Browning story, and, even more incredibly, not only their names but their academic titles. One gets the uncanny feeling that these professors and so on, who are cited or confuted, are living at the same historic time as the Brownings and their circle, and partaking of their lives. In one instance, it even appears that Elizabeth Barrett and Robert Browning are somehow accompanied closely in their love-affair, elopement, and honeymoon, not merely by a College Dean, but, as would appear from the text that names him, no less than a Dean Emeritus. Such absurdities are perhaps an unwelcome feature of the otherwise admirable record of our achievements in biography in the twentieth century.

3
Paths of Progress

I have suggested that the sheer weight of evidence now available to the biographer does not necessarily make a successful biography, but may even handicap that achievement. This is evident in attempting to look at some of the main developments likely in biographies of the future. As a biographer practising here and now, I do not pretend that many of these will be more than guesswork on my part. If a theme emerges in this guesswork it is, I hope, that the nature of biography is to be, within formal limits, infinitely adaptable. That is practically a definition of poetry also, and I should wish to suggest that biography and poetry, with their intense humanistic interests, now have more in common than has yet been generally recognized.

However, to return to the theme of the weight of the evidence: this, with its verbal aids of tape-recording, its visual aids of telerecording, xerox, and microfilm, its global documentation of every aspect of life, would seem to give the biographer huge and unexplored possibilities of arriving at accuracy. Yet in fact, as is well known generally, and specially to those of us who have worked professionally in radio or television, these media have often had a disastrous effect on evidence. One has only to see or hear a so-called confrontation between two famous people, or an apparently frank statement by a single one of them, to know that the caution imposed by consciousness of the vast possible audience has reduced such discussions and such statements to meaninglessness. The art of concealment has become paramount, the exercise of saying nothing at all has been carried to the finest possible point. That is one handicap to all future research. The other is the innocent faking – and one must stress the word 'innocent' – that afflicts all forms of public documentation. To give a concrete example, there is a personal one told by a man who for some years held a post in the Military Secretariat of the British War Cabinet. The years of his office were some of the most important in the whole history of British Government; they brought him in contact with persons, Churchill and others, whose actual words would be invaluable to any biographer, in the years during and just after the last war. The Cabinet minutes, when released, would seem to get as near the truth about the personalities involved, statesmen, generals, administrators, as anything could do. Alas, that truth will never be known, owing to the method of recording these minutes, which this assistant secretary has explained as his almost daily job. First, his function was to take down by shorthand or notes what the ministers, or those summoned to advise them actually said. Like all human discussion, perhaps especially in time of stress, this was virtually without form, incoherent, illogical, illiterate, and frequently inconclusive. It was therefore the function of this official, a trained academic scholar as well as a civil servant, to rewrite the whole affair, and give it the form it ought to have taken, to substitute in order, logic, and expression what he judged the participants had meant to say, not what they actually did say: for example, to make sense of a well-known explosive British general, who was so impatient of mere words that he often said China when he meant Russia, or Italy when he meant Germany: and so on. Yet the process of this innocent faking did not stop there. If the assistant secretary, at the next Cabinet meeting, had read back as minutes those beautifully composed and logically ordered conversations, the speakers would have recognized so little of the speeches now assigned to them that they would refuse to accept them as a true record. He therefore had to introduce a sufficient amount of illogicality, human failing, and, above all, conventional diction, to persuade the members of a British Cabinet that this was what they might each one conceivably have said. The finished result, the final article of the future biographer's so-called evidence, is therefore at least two removes away from anything that was actually said and that actually happened. This must apply now to the proceedings of so many institutions anywhere, all over the world. Happy and lucky is the biographer such as Roy Jenkins, whose elevation to the affairs of the European Economic Community must be regarded, in one sense, as a loss to English biography. He discovered, and was allowed to use, the notes which a British Prime Minister in the first half of the First World War, Mr Asquith, used to scribble during Cabinet meetings, notes which his colleagues thought showed the Prime Minister's close attention to his job. They were in fact letters, sometimes two or three a day, to Asquith's girl-friend, describing for her benefit exactly what went on in the Cabinet, who said what and why, full of accurate and often satirical description of the doings and even looks of people like Lloyd George.

Such a find unfortunately, in these days of multiple concealment, is no longer likely to come the biographer's way. The danger is that he or she will take the carefully manoeuvred and stage-managed telefilm for the event, the skilfully edited and adapted tape for the words really spoken, all that has been officially and formally sanctified as the fact which occurred. Once more, it is not the mass and variety of evidence which counts, but its quality, reliability, and relevance to the subject. Professor John A. Garraty, in his book *The Nature of Biography*, has a tongue-in-cheek picture of the writing of one of those innumerable lives of Abraham Lincoln by a biographer attempting to use the overwhelming if irrelevant types of aid to biography now available. According to Professor Garraty

> *In writing* Abraham Lincoln: the War Years, *Carl Sandburg used besides conventional sources, pictures, cartoons, posters, and other unusual materials. He bought hundreds of books containing Lincolniana and tore them apart, extracting the pages he considered pertinent for his work.*

One should interpolate that Sandburg today would have photocopied pages, but the principle is the same. Professor Garraty continues the story.

> *These, together with his other notes, he tacked to an upright screen set next to a large biscuit tin, which supported his typewriter. He was assisted by two copyists and by his wife and three daughters, who filed and organized material. He worked in the attic of his home, surrounded by masses of books. In fine weather this paraphernalia was transferred to the yard, where Sandburg, clad only in a green eye-shade, a loin-cloth and sandals, typed away in the midst of his flock of pedigreed goats.*

This sounds, without satire, like any modern biographer trying to deal with his overwhelming material, though not all of us may have the advantages of two copyists, a wife, three daughters, and a flock of pedigreed goats. The point is that all of what Garraty calls 'unusual materials' can only be used with due caution. The pictures seen by the subject of a biography are entirely relevant; but care must be taken that we are seeing what was genuinely seen at the time. For many years, biographers denied that Titian's *Bacchus and Ariadne* could have influenced Keats's Ode in the fourth book of *Endymion*. Where were 'the light blue hills' of the poem? The answer was that they were hidden under what the Victorians called a rich impasto of protective varnish. In our time, this has been removed by modern cleaning and the biographer can now see in the National Gallery in London exactly what Keats saw, and the colours he put into his poem. The picture in its new guise gives one a delighted shock; we are literally seeing with Keats's eyes. To take, though, an opposite example, such posters as those used by Sandburg as his biographical material can be totally misleading as contemporary evidence. To judge by advertising posters of Hardy ale, you would think that Thomas Hardy was a hearty drinker. In point of fact, he was nearly a teetotaller, his name and picture simply being used by a local brewery to advertise its new super-strong ale.

At the same time it is true that modern biography does choose, and future biographers may be expected to choose, not only unorthodox sources, but unorthodox subjects. Faced with the huge, complex, and possibly misleading archives of orthodox documentation, faced with numerous large-scale biographies of all the major and many of the minor figures of human history, the biographer may seek to illuminate human life, which, after all, is the prime aim, by using unexpected sources for unusual people. If so, it will at least be a relief for the general reader. We are surely at a stage where Jefferson, Lincoln, Washington, Nelson, Wellington, Queen Victoria, and other monoliths can hardly stand another touch from the biographic sculptor. How much a minor subject can illuminate, how unexpected the sources may be, is illustrated by a recent life-study by the Regius Professor of History at Oxford, Hugh Trevor-Roper. Trevor-Roper, author of a distinguished youthful biography of Archbishop Laud, received a few years ago a somewhat odd request. In Trevor-Roper's own words,

In the summer of 1973, a distinguished Swiss scientist, director of an international medical institute, wrote to me, in somewhat guarded terms, asking me whether I would receive, and, if I thought fit, transmit to the Bodleian Library for preservation there, a substantial work . . . which had recently come into his hands. In explanation of his request, my correspondent enclosed a history of the document and the written opinions of two distinguished scholars. These scholars agreed that it was of great literary and historical value, although it was clear, from their reports, that it was also somewhat obscene.

In view of this last impression, Trevor-Roper was not surprised when this document was not entrusted to the post, but was ceremoniously given to him by hand at Basle airport, where he happened to land on a journey. His suspicion about the contents was proved an underestimate. It was the manuscript autobiography of an obscure Englishman in the 1890s and 1900s, who claimed, among much else, to have had sexual relations with a most extraordinary selection of famous people all over the world, ranging from the dowager Empress of China to a distinguished British Prime Minister. Trevor-Roper, as a trained historian, was soon able to satisfy himself that all this was a huge sexual fantasy, but, at the same time, extremely cleverly put together. A sexual relationship with the poet Verlaine, for example, was based on an actual one between the poet and someone else, neatly fitted into what was then an unknown space of time in Verlaine's life-story. Yet even in disposing of all this, what fascinated Trevor-Roper was that this man, who had spent a good deal of his life in China, seemed to show not only intimate and accurate knowledge of the Chinese Imperial Court, but surprisingly, of the British Foreign Office in the First World War, a large Scottish international ship-building firm, and the American Bank Note Company. Pursuing all this now as a matter of biographical research, Trevor-Roper examined the past records of all these institutions, receiving special help from the present-day officials of the American Bank

Note Company. What emerged, briefly, was that all these bodies had been, at one time or another, massively swindled by the writer of the autobiography. He had sold the British Government, in deep need in the armament crisis of 1915, 200,000 non-existent rifles, transported in a non-existent flotilla of non-existent ships. He had forged a contract for seven battleships between the Chinese Government and the Scottish shipping firm of John Brown, for whom he acted as agent. Finally, he had negotiated for the American Bank Note Company a totally fictitious deal with the Chinese Government for one hundred million Chinese banknotes. The light this threw on the British Foreign Office, in desperate wartime straits, a hard-headed shipping company anxious to make its profit out of the modernization of China, and the even more hardheaded agents of a huge American Corporation, scenting a big deal with a new government, was immense. Trevor-Roper, taking this obscure man, officially known only as a benefactor to the Bodleian of some Chinese manuscripts, which may or may not be genuine, produced a biography which is also a startling piece of world social history, in his book *A Hidden Life: the Enigma of Sir Edmund Backhouse*.

Such is one type of biography we may look for in the future. This is not to suggest that a biography is valid simply because the subject is obscure, scandalous, or eccentric, though that type of writing, as we saw, is at least as old as the eighteenth-century biography of the scholar John North by his brother. It is rather that a fruitful field lies in biography of an obscure person, who by some fortune is connected with important events or institutions, and whose history throws an unexpected, revealing light on these. Trevor-Roper's study illuminates the dealings of the British Government, and the workings of western business with the emerging Far East, through a personal study of the warped but fascinating manoeuvres of one person's extraordinary life and conduct.

There is, however, warning as well as encouragement for future biographers in this brilliantly successful book. It will be noticed that the sexual fantasy-life of the subject, which intrigued Trevor-Roper and others initially as readers, was rejected by him as a conscientious biographer. It is often said that the sexual freedom of modern times, especially the verbal freedom now enjoyed by literature, theatre, film, novels, and perhaps most of all by autobiography, will immensely enlarge the scope of later biography. For example, Christopher Isherwood's latest autobiography tells us in the frankest terms about the sexual life of himself and his contemporaries in the 1930s. It reveals in so many words what his more discreet colleague W. H. Auden said in his poem –

Who goes with who
The bedclothes say

As I and you
Go kissed away

Will such things, then, not add a completely new dimension to biography? If I seem doubtful, it is not through any pretence that such things do not matter. They emphatically do. The trouble is, they can so often be proved untrue. One lesson every biographer learns is that people's capacity for sexual fantasy is unlimited, but can often be exploded by the simplest means. To take one isolated example: Brendan Bracken, Minister of Information in Churchill's war government, let it be believed, and indeed encouraged the belief, that he was Winston Churchill's bastard son. In view of the favour and indeed affection shown by Churchill to this talented but somewhat untutored man, this was generally accepted; but directly an expert biographer dealt with it, the whole fantasy disappeared. Andrew Boyle, Bracken's biographer, simply consulted the Public Record Office in Dublin, and found Bracken legitimately born in Tipperary to two Catholic Irish parents in February 1901. He was therefore presumably conceived about May 1900, a time when Churchill, several thousand miles away, was a war correspondent in the South African War. The whole thing was a fantasy of a kind only too well-known to biographers, that of attaching to any public figure some intriguing but impossible sexual anecdote.

Yet even more misleading to the modern biographer are the sexual fantasies concocted about people by their earlier biographers. When I first started working on a biography of Keats, I found a settled biographical tradition that Keats, in his short life, had no sexual experience. This seemed unlikely in a virile young man of the Regency period, a medical student whose hospital lecturers assumed that all their students had such experiences, a writer who used sexual terms freely and familiarly in letters and even in his poems. I found the legend began with one particular biographer and editor, Sidney Colvin. Colvin refused ever to print Keats's passionate though discreetly expressed letters to his fiancée, Fanny Brawne. He cut out of Keats's other letters all expressions of what Colvin called 'mere crudity' – meaning sex. It was not that Colvin did not understand these passages. Far from it. At Harvard, examining Keats's autograph letters, I found such words, when indistinct in Keats's own often hasty hand, were pencilled over in another hand, making the sexual word or joke clear. The pencilled hand was that of the editor, Colvin himself, who then proceeded to omit the passage, whose meaning he obviously knew only too well. In my *John Keats* I printed a glossary of these contemporary sexual expressions used by the poet, and very hot water I got into for doing so. Nurtured on Colvin's standard biography, people simply would not believe that the words meant what they did. Keats's admirers preferred to believe that the poet, meticulous in his use of words, was writing gibberish rather than showing sexual knowledge.

Yet if what the biographer Isaac Walton would have called 'this overlong digression' seems to say that biography should not be left to prudish professors, let us at once hail a professor, Gordon N. Ray of Yale, who has made a love-affair into a splendid double biography. The double biography of a relationship, which throws light on both characters, is a fruitful development of modern life-writing. Professor Ray was allowed to use at Yale the voluminous letters of H. G. Wells to Rebecca West, which detailed almost day by day the ten-year love-affair of these two great twentieth-century authors. Ray overcomes the severe handicap of having only one side of the correspondence, Wells's, and the daunting fact that Dame Rebecca is still alive, with tact, accuracy, sympathy, and clarity. Moreover his study, *H. G. Wells and Rebecca West*, throws great light both on the literary history and the social mores of their time. He makes their lovers' talk – they called each other Jaguar and Panther, two cats – amusing and real. It is one of the best examples of this new genre of dual biography, of which, perhaps, the perfect modern example is the book by Cecil Woodham-Smith, whose recent death is such a loss to biography, entitled *The Reason Why*. Mrs Woodham-Smith's book explained for the first time why, in the Crimean War, the famous and fatal charge of the Light Brigade, immortalized in Tennyson's poem, ever took place.

To do this, she wrote what is virtually a double biography, a joint life of two English military commanders, Lord Lucan and Lord Cardigan. The lives
of both of them, before they became associated in the
Crimean War, had been entangled with one another
in the most dramatic and disastrous ways. Both were
men of exceptionally difficult temperament. As Mrs
Woodham-Smith outlines this double life-story, one
watches with a kind of helpless horror these two lives
converging towards one fatal moment. The men had
clashed before, and it was inevitable that, if they
clashed again, it would have dire results. It did; and
the occasion was an ambiguous order issued by their
commander-in-chief, the vague and elderly Lord
Raglan. In the words of Mrs Woodham-Smith, which
typify the biographer's art of catching the focal
moment among the thousands that make up a human
story,

> *Meanwhile Lord Lucan, almost for the first time, was
> speaking directly and personally to Lord Cardigan. Had
> the two men not detested each other so bitterly, had they
> been able to examine the order together and discuss its
> meaning, the Light Brigade might have been saved.
> Alas, thirty years of hatred could not be bridged.*

The dramatic impact of this kind of dual biography is
immense. It is in dramatic writing too that modern
biography excels. In this, the popular media, television

and others, may have played a beneficent part. To take a quotation from the same book, there is hardly any passage in biography to equal in modern, dramatic realism, Mrs Woodham-Smith's account of the death of Captain Nolan, who had brought the fatal ambiguous order to the two commanders.

> *Nolan . . . turning in his saddle, shouted and waved his sword as if he would address the Brigade, but the guns were firing with great crashes, and not a word could be heard. Had he suddenly realised that . . . he had directed the Light Brigade to certain death? No one will ever know, because at that moment a Russian shell burst on the right of Lord Cardigan, and a fragment tore its way into Nolan's breast, exposing the heart. The sword fell from his hand, but his right arm was still erect, and his body remained rigid in the saddle. His horse wheeled and began to gallop back through the advancing Brigade, and then from the body there burst a strange and appalling cry, a shriek so unearthly as to freeze the blood of all who heard him. The terrified horse carried the body, still shrieking, through the 4th Light Dragoons, and then at last Nolan fell from the saddle, dead.*

That level of biographical writing surely reaches the heights of dramatic artistry. It gets another dimension of art too because it is true. We know those men died under those guns. The scientific search for truth has been translated into sheer artistic triumph. Desmond

McCarthy may have reminded us that a biographer is an artist, but an artist on oath; yet the oath has aided the art. It is the poet's search for truth through his art. It confirms what we suggested earlier: that the art of the biographer has very much in common with the art and pursuit of the poet.

How then shall we estimate the type of modern biography produced by methods which have much more in common with modern scientific research, the life-study resulting from a team of scholars working together like a team of scientists, on different aspects of topics in some large-scale central archive? A biography such as that of Sir Winston Churchill can be produced in such a way, and perhaps in no other. The complexities of the vast archival material involved can perhaps only be solved by a team of experts, political, social, economic, each one taking responsibility for his or her own aspect of the subject. This too seems an almost inevitable development of modern biography, but again one which has its peculiar dangers. It may well become supremely accurate, but at the same time disappointingly impersonal. Biography, however objective in method, must have somewhere the personal touch, since it deals essentially with personal life, even when its subject is very much a public figure.

There is one important modern development, though, which is almost the opposite of this process. It is when one person writes what is virtually a multiple set of small biographies, adding up to the whole life of a community. This, the extension of the dual biography into what we may call multibiography, is best exemplified over the past few years by Ronald Blythe's *Akenfield*. As has become well-known through its film and television versions, this is a factual picture of an English village community, by means of dozens of small-scale biographies, accompanied by edited tape-recorded conversations, spoken by the subjects of these biographies. It is not, it must be emphasized, simple reportage, where the tapes alone are left to speak. These brief biographies, like Aubrey's seventeenth-century brief lives, are written with insight into character, with very considerable research into each person's life. The tapes when transcribed simply illustrate, in a forceful way, these life sketches. Such multibiographies are the culmination of one of the chief movements which we have seen, from the biography of people notable in the world's eye to ordinarily unregarded persons. Ronald Blythe's achievement in *Akenfield* is not so much the picture that emerges of a hard-working community, though that seems to have been his editorial aim, but that numerous people emerge as individuals, and as interesting, lively, and sometimes deeply moving characters. 'The short and simple annals of the poor,' in the poet's phrase, turn out to be neither so short nor so simple. This type of multibiography verges, of course, on social history, and will be used as the material for historical study. Yet it exists in its own right as what seems to be a new

84

form, presented by Blythe with great, and in this case, local insight, yet given a personal stamp by his skilful linking of these small biographies to one another.

This important question of personal as against impersonal interpretation is one which a modern biographer particularly has to face. However much objective data one accumulates, by team effort or by isolated research, a biography is always apt to be more than an exploration of one's subject; it becomes, at every step, an exploration of oneself. Many people have started by writing biography, and found that this has led them to be effectively writing their own autobiography. Autobiography, though naturally very closely related to biography, presents its own special problems. It is perhaps most successful when it is achieved by this indirect way, emerging almost unconsciously, from an attempt to write an intimate biography. I mentioned Christopher Isherwood's recent autobiography. Yet to my mind, a far more convincing picture of the author appears in his study, *Kathleen and Frank*, a dual biography of his own parents. It embodies not only an age and a social class in English history, but also an objective, sincere self-examination of the youth of the writer himself. Autobiography needs perpetually to be purged of self-consciousness; and this can be done by such a shift of view. Some autobiography, too, may prove the best biography of someone closely connected with the author. Perhaps the most remarkable instance of this is the picture of the

First World War poet, Wilfred Owen, drawn in the autobiography of his brother, Harold Owen. This autobiography is called *Journey From Obscurity*; and the 'obscurity' of Harold Owen was caused by the intense maternal concentration by their mother on the success of her favourite elder son Wilfred. In fact, so extreme was this, that the education of Harold, writer of the autobiography, was so far neglected that to the end of his days he wrote only in capital letters, like a young child, never in lower case, and even, to the dismay of his bank manager, made his signature in easily forged capitalizations. One can imagine, too, the feelings of publishers on receiving a long manuscript, hand-written in capitals. Be that as it may, the autobiography was published, and was widely successful, for two main reasons. One was that Harold Owen was a talented but an entirely unprofessional and untaught author. There was no professional and literary glossy surface to these memoirs; they were the simple revelation itself. The second was that they were indirectly a unique biography of his brother the poet, written with family candour but with complete and convincing charity, a lesson in life-study.

Biography, then, is partly self-examination. Problems of judgement may depend on self-knowledge. How to judge, for example – if indeed at all – a Beethoven whose music grew more and more to approach the divine, and whose personal life became increasingly petty and sordid. We can hardly deal with this unless we have attempted to appraise such tendencies, to a lesser degree, in our own personalities. Hardy's dying action was to dictate two mean, inept, and unworthy sets of doggerel verses about two critics who had offended him, George Moore and G. K. Chesterton. Yet how can we judge what might occur in the mind of an 87-year-old man without some self-knowledge of what might possibly go on in our own brain if we manage to reach that age? And yet too, some judgement, implicit if not explicit, must be conveyed to the readers, unless we are simply to give them an insipid diet of fact without comment.

In fact one of the dangers of biography, and I use the word 'danger' without exaggeration, is that it may well become too self-searching for the biographer's own good. There is an interesting parable about this in the work of a neglected thinker, a philosopher and pioneer ecologist of the nineteen-thirties, Olaf Stapledon. *Last and First Men,* among his many other writings, provided an early example of non-sensational science fiction. More convincingly than many later authors, because writing in uncompromisingly matter-of-fact, determinedly non-literary style, Stapledon imagines a future for the human race which involves its near-extinction no less than twenty-two times in a time-span of billions of years, and which covers mass-migrations to two other planets. The parable he creates is one concerning what he calls the Fifth Men, the race which will inhabit this earth when

our race of First Men has caused the virtual holocaust
which will practically, though not quite, render Man
extinct, and when three more races of Men have simi-
larly been extinguished. These Fifth Men, after endur-
ing their own troubles and vicissitudes, emerge as
potentially a finer, more talented, and more sensitive
civilization than ours has ever been. Unfortunately, in
this Pandora-like legend, told with factual, straight-
faced economy, they have an ultra-sympathetic
curiosity about their past, which, of course, stretches
back to our present. In search of this, they develop a
sixth sense, an historical time-sense, which enables
them to know and feel exactly what our lives were
like. They become, as it were, super-biographers. The
results, sketched by Stapledon's irony, are a disaster
for them. The clue to past ages becomes the key to
their own despair. In their sophisticated innocence, it
has never occurred to them that history, 'the essence of
innumerable biographies', in Carlyle's words, may also
be, in Gibbon's words, 'little more than the register
of the crimes, follies, and misfortunes of mankind'.
By entering totally into our lives, they become convinced that even the best and noblest efforts of existence are doomed to ultimate disaster. They apply the
sad lesson of such multiple biography to their
own lives. This leaves them convinced that even their
own best achievements hold within them the seeds of
inevitable self-destruction. Their studies in biography
turn to such morbid self-criticism that they almost

despair and are about to commit virtual race-suicide when they are diverted by an alteration in the solar system, which makes it necessary for them to develop space-travel, and colonize another planet.

Stapledon's fiction, logically extended in this way, is one experienced in fact by all conscientious practitioners of biography. Few past lives are happy, fulfilled, and ultimately satisfying. The despairs and defeated ambitions of former men and women tend to become the despairs and doubts of our own lives. They even make us doubt what we are doing in their exploration. To some, one can imagine, biography could become a self-defeating art. Truth can be lethal. Human life thrives on healthy illusion. Yet if I have sometimes dwelt on the difficulties, the pains and necessary penalties of biography, it is time to conclude with the biographer's rewards and encouragements. One feature of this relatively modern profession is the storming by women of the citadel of biography. Longer delayed than women's advance as novelists, it has now become one of the most vitalizing factors in life-writing. Though at first confined largely, with a few seventeenth-century exceptions, to women writing *about* women – one thinks of the perceptive lives there have been not only of Charlotte Brontë, but of Anne, of Emily Brontë too, culminating in the triumphant trilogy by Winifred Gérin – it is now true to say that women seem to have achieved better than men the difficult art of extending imaginative sympathy into the viewpoint of another sex. Perhaps Winifred Gérin's finest work, in fact, was not her exploration of the secret world of the Brontë sisters, but her companion volume on their far more difficult brother, Branwell. Recent biographies by women writers have dealt with complex male characters in a spirit of understanding and realistic charity, which has produced some outstanding examples.

Women biographers have found themselves particularly adept in disentangling the mixed-up masculine heroes of the British nineteenth century, those strange maintainers of Britain's short-lived Empire. To take one among many, the Reverend Charles Kingsley, mostly known for his classic children's book, *The Water Babies*, and for the phrase he himself invented, 'muscular Christianity', offered a challenge to any biographer. Almost a caricature of the hearty Englishman, who certainly hastened his own death by throwing open his bedroom windows in mid-winter during a North American lecture tour, Kingsley presented even more complicated biographical puzzles. It might daunt anybody to portray this devout Victorian clergyman, who, far from believing that in the Kingdom of Heaven there was neither marriage nor giving in marriage, stated that in the life hereafter marital sex would be enjoyed to a greater degree than ever on earth, and even made pen-and-ink drawings showing himself and his most attractive wife ascending to heaven in the nude and in full action. The solution of how to present Kingsley, in this and many other highly individual ideas, with sympathy, and not merely as a notable English eccentric, is the achievement of a very recent biography by Susan Chitty, embellished, one must add, by Kingsley's own most original illustrations. Mrs Chitty succeeds in giving us Kingsley not as some psychological freak, but as a real and even understandable character.

In the last few years, there has been example after example of difficult male characters portrayed with understanding by women biographers, Oliver Cromwell and Wellington in the specially difficult spheres of military leadership and social and religious character, Patrick Pearse the Irish revolutionary, Burne-Jones, an artist whose work and character, and indeed whole psychological make-up has so far eluded discovery. One can say that whatever pockets of sex-discrimination may remain, the profession of the biographer is not one of them, and that both public and fellow authors have acclaimed these successes.

This is one with the general acclaim biography has gained, by whomsoever written, even over the last decade. Biography is no longer viewed as a kind of poor relation or adjunct to either literature or history. The idea of character as a historical force has been established, whatever one may think of Tolstoi's playing-down of the idea. The idea that biography cannot illuminate literature has also gone by the board, in the face of the revelations that exact biographical knowledge of artists has made in the appreciation of their art, and the exact way in which they, poet, painter, musician, produced it, and what their meaning and motive was in doing so. Biography can not only illuminate and extend our knowledge of the creative process, but also save us from factual mistakes in criticism, though there is still a tendency in some literary criticism to isolate the creation from the creator, and thus frequently to miss the obvious in criticism.

It is the exhilaration of modern biography to find how common sense and close to life it has become. In this progress, from the pious, celebratory, and lauda-tory, we seem to have arrived at a notable point when present life itself is enlarged and enriched by what we read about past lives. Biography has attained more than respectability as a study. It is even academically recog-nized, in many schools and colleges, as a subject in its own right. Courses are taught, and students gain credits purely in biography. Yet one would not put academic status as the ultimate in the development of biography. Biography is a highly individual concern. One cannot lay down rules or formulate aesthetic judgements. Every biography is a matter between the biographer and subject, each one highly personal. This perhaps is its final fascination. It is often said, rather loosely, that it is somehow like criminal detection; but the biographic detective is working on a different assumption from the criminal one. It is assumed that all life has something worth recording, and recording truly for all time. The search for this truth assumes that the truth about men and women is totally desirable, helpful, and important, no matter what the result of the investigation. That is why biography, and the exploration of human life, in all its strength and frailty, will continue to grow, beyond its relatively short past history, to one of the leading features of the creative output of future generations. This at all events is finally the faith of one biographer.

Select Bibliography

A. H. Clough (rev. and ed.), *Plutarch's Lives*

T. More, *Richard the Third*

R. S. Sylvester and D. P. Harding (eds.), *Two Early Tudor Lives (The Life and Death of Cardinal Wolsey*, George Cavendish; *The Life of Sir Thomas More,* William Roper)★

I. Walton, *Lives*

O. Lawson Dick (ed. and sel.), *Aubrey's Brief Lives*★

R. North, *Lives of . . . John North*

S. Johnson, *Lives of English Poets*★

J. Boswell, *Life of Dr Samuel Johnson*★

T. Carlyle, *Life of Frederick the Great*★

E. C. Gaskell, *Life of Charlotte Bronte*★

L. Strachey, *Eminent Victorians*★

P. Green, *Kenneth Grahame*

E. P. Thompson, *William Morris, from Romantic to Revolutionary*★

H. Nicholson, *George the Fifth*

G. M. Trevelyan, *Garibaldi*

J. Manton, *Sister Dora*★

J. A. Garraty, *The Nature of Biography*

H. Trevor-Roper, *A Hidden Life (Hermit of Peking*★)

G. N. Ray, *H. G. Wells and Rebecca West*

C. Woodham-Smith, *The Reason Why*★

R. Jenkins, *Mr Asquith*

R. Blythe, *Akenfield*★

H. Owen, *Journey from Obscurity*

W. Gérin, *Charlotte Brontë*★

O. Stapledon, *Last and First Men*★

S. Chitty, *Charles Kingsley's Landscape*

★ available in paperback

Index

ROBERT GITTINGS

is best known for his work on Keats and Hardy, including the much acclaimed biographies *John Keats, Young Thomas Hardy* and *The Older Hardy*.

He was born in Portsmouth in 1911, and educated at St. Edward's School, Oxford, and Jesus College, Cambridge, where he was Scholar, Research Student, and then Fellow and Supervisor of Studies.

Between 1940 and 1963 Dr. Gittings was a producer and writer of features and educational scripts for the BBC. Since then he has been a Visiting Professor at several universities in the USA, most recently at the University of Washington in Seattle, where he gave the lectures on which *The Nature of Biography* is based. He has had many volumes of his own verse and verse dramas published over the past forty years.

Robert Gittings has received many literary and academic awards. These include the W. H. Smith Literary Award, 1969, for *John Keats*; and the Phi Beta Kappa Christian Gauss Award in Literary Scholarship and Criticism for *Young Thomas Hardy*.